The author conducts inservices, workshops and speaking engagements on the following topics.

These are a few examples:

- Why people come to the United States
- Why millions of foreigners don't come through the so-called "the front door"
- What it means to be illegal
- What it's like to be the child of an undocumented immigrant
- Why English is still the main language of the USA
- The advantages of being fluent in another language
- Is it realistic to expect American adults to become fluent in another language?
- Why don't American schools produce second-language speakers?
- Preparing kids for the international world that is right here
- What's right or wrong about being mad at immigrants?
- The cost of coming to America
- Behind the scenes of Max and Max Spanish videos
- Do we really understand Latino immigrants?
- Mistakes that immigrants make
- How immigrants can and should win the hearts of citizens
- What do I need to know about dating immigrants?
- What lovers need to know about fraudulent marriages

To book Max T. for an event, call 317-731-2629

No matter how many illegal immigrants continue crossing the border, Spanish is a dying language in the United States. It is dying household by household. It will not totally die out, but Latinos are switching to English fast, just as other immigrant populations have. People who want to reach the Latinos need to quit fighting for the survival of the English language. More people speak English every year than ever before.

Spanish is a Dying Language

How Businesses, Organizations, and Politicians Can Reach Latinos

Max T. Russell

ISBN-10: 1491214120
ISBN-13: 978-1491214121

DEDICATION

A mi cuñada, Carolina, quien ya se cansa
de ser llamada inmigrante.
Es una mera norteamericana – y toda una latina.

To my sister-in-law, Carolina, who is tired of
being called an immigrant.
She's just a regular American girl – and totally Latina.

CONTENTS

THE DEATH OF GERMAN

In 2001 I decided to undertake a project that would fund leadership development among inner-city males between the ages of about 15 and 40. I wondered what kind of project could produce the money needed for that. *I know*, I said to myself, *I'll make software to help adults learn a limited amount of useful Spanish*. It seemed like a good idea, because people in businesses and organizations were always asking me if I could teach them Spanish or recommend a learning program. I didn't have time to personally teach them, and I didn't want to.

I was convinced that there must be at least several million adults in this country who were ready and raring to learn Spanish.

Several years and many observations later, I realized that those adults were never going to speak much of another language. What they wanted was to be able to connect to the Spanish-speaking Latinos. That meant they needed to know what I know about the Latinos. A billion times I had crossed the gaps they wanted to cross. Language didn't need to stand in their way. Neither did politics.

I had been led down a winding, confusing path by monolingual Americans who *thought* they would become fluent in Spanish, if they could just get their hands on the right learning program. My project took unexpected twists and turns as I tried to respond to the FACT that the adults were not going to learn the language. Meanwhile, America kept changing…to their benefit.

1

Whatever happened to the German language?

A high school German teacher told me he was switching to teaching Spanish.

"You are?" I said.

"Sure," he replied. "Nobody needs German anymore."

It's easy to forget that German immigrants in the U.S. increased by millions between 1850 and 1930, and yet hardly anyone in this country speaks German anymore. Even by 1930 German as a primary language here had decreased at supersonic speed. One high school after another continues dropping the language from its curriculum. Even if German were taught in every high school in the country, it would still be dead in this country. School does not keep a language alive.

My mother's parents were German, spoke the language, spoke it to each other when they didn't want the kids to understand them, and didn't pass it on to them. They had nine children and none of them spoke German. Neither do any of us grandkids. It's the same for many, many millions of German descendants, including those whose ancestors came to the U.S. before 1850 or after 1930.

Just yesterday I met a woman from the Netherlands who has lived in America for 40 years. She said she can't get rid of her foreign accent but she has trouble remembering some of her first language, because she doesn't speak it nearly as much as she speaks English. She met some other Dutch women who still speak German, and now the group meets fairly regularly to talk the language with each other.

"German is dead in the U.S.," I said.

"Oh, yes," she replied. "My son understands German, but he won't answer me in German."

"His kids won't speak German," I said.

"No," she said, "they won't."

It's true that the Amish have remained separate from what they call "English" society and have preserved derivatives of German. But the language is dead in American society.

If you're taking one of those "learn German the natural way" programs, be sure to take a trip to Germany afterward so you can experience firsthand how it feels to try your German on your peers there, only to find that they prefer to speak your language than to inch through conversation with you in theirs. That's just one of a hundred such language cases.

Could it happen to Spanish?

When I first told my wife that fewer and fewer Latinos would be speaking Spanish as a primary language, she said, "I can already see it happening. I go into the Mexican restaurant and the workers are talking like me."

Think about that before you make all kinds of plans to become bilingual or to gear your business or organization up for Spanish-speaking clientele. Keep the changing times in perspective. I've been collecting information firsthand from immigrants all over the country for more than 30 years. All is not what it appears to be.

If you are not fluent by now, it is almost certain that you never will be. After all, not even one percent of students become fluent in the language they study. Things have been this way for more than a century. But even if you can't enjoy the powerful benefits that come with speaking Spanish, you can take advantage of the big change that has gone unseen by most businesses.

Immigrants are adopting English as their primary language

Latino immigrants BY THE MILLIONS are learning English better every day. In fact, millions of them already speak English better than Spanish. And many no longer even speak Spanish, if they ever did. Here are some observations that come to mind:

- More Latinos are asking me to speak English to them. They say to me in English while I'm speaking Spanish, "Do you speak English? It's easier for me."

3

- Many Latinos know English before they get here. Immigrants from Latin America come here already knowing English—maybe three languages.
- Latino leaders, immigration attorneys, and marketers are encouraging immigrants to speak YOUR language. The children of these immigrants are learning English in school, but mostly by hanging around fluent English-speaking kids and listening to a flood of English-language media. It's a plain fact: more Latinos are speaking less Spanish and more English.
- If two immigrants marry and have four children, those four children are almost certain to make English their primary language. Even if the parents were to resist learning English, the family would be 67% English-speaking. That's a pretty important piece of information for marketing, especially considering that so many parents use their kids as interpreters.

A language begins to die within two generations. Immigrant parents struggle to preserve their first language even to the second generation. An astounding number of children answer in English when parents speak to them in Spanish. This is true for other languages too.

These children prefer that you communicate with them in English.

They may or may not read Spanish. Most read English far better.

Don't think that school keeps a language alive. I checked on a Cherokee school district that has been trying to revive the old language and culture, and they are pulling their hair out. There's not enough time in the school day, the preparation hours are too long for the language teachers, hardly anyone actually speaks the language anymore—since most of the ones who did are dead and gone—and the tattoos and longer hair that are part of the attempted cultural revival aren't going to motivate the young Cherokee to learn the difficult language that is breathing its last.

Languages die every year in Latin America and around the world. Mexico has 300 languages, for example, and each year fewer people speak them. The native speakers are dying while Spanish continues as the primary language of that country. The languages eventually get to the place where they have only five speakers, then four, three, two, one, and poof!

Fifteen percent of Peru's population is Quechua, but each year more members of that population are preferring to speak Spanish instead of

Quechua. Many of the children deny that they can speak Quechua. They look me straight in the face and say, in Quechua-accented, broken Spanish, "No, I don't speak Quechua." Even some adult Quechua insist they only speak Spanish, while their Quechua syllables and accent come screaming through.

Some native speakers of any language insist that they will never forget their language. I promise them they will if they do not use it. They don't believe me. As time goes by, these people merge into society beyond their ethnic neighborhoods, and the language begins to quietly slip away. Eventually the realization of loss dawns on the once fluent speakers. After several years, speaking the language requires so much effort that they automatically fall into a pattern of using English as often as possible.

That is the way of language. You'd be surprised how many Spanish-speaking Latinos here in the States can't get their kids to keep Spanish in the family. The kids often just don't have any interest in it. They're too absorbed in merging into the dominant culture. When I spoke with a group of Hispanic (or Latino) students who formed a Hispanic Club at their college, they spoke to me in perfect English. I had to speak English to be sure all of them understood me. NONE OF THEM spoke Spanish to each other. And those are students in the heart of a Latino community.

The progression from Spanish to English is at different points everywhere in the United States, but it is happening on a national scale. You are wise to give it careful consideration. As I write this, I realize it is even truer than the last time I stopped to think about it, **even though illegal immigration continues**.

So...

To all the people in businesses and organizations who wonder how to build relationships with the Latino immigrants you see moving into your towns, and who know down deep that you're never going to speak much Spanish, I wrote this book specifically for you.

Whoever wants to connect their business or organization with the Latino community must understand what makes immigrants tick. Immigrants face challenges, priorities and concerns that place them in a group not well understood by others. That's what I'll talk about in the next chapter.

WHO ARE THE LATINOS?

Latinos come from many nations and do not appreciate being lumped into one nationality. A Dominican is a Dominican, and a Chilean is a Chilean. Unlike what many U.S. citizens think, everyone with brown skin, dark features, and who speaks Spanish is not from Mexico. Millions of Latinos are white. Furthermore, not everyone in Mexico is very similar to other Mexicans. Countries have distinct regional variety, and the variety can be quite drastic. I find that most Latinos don't know very much about the different regions of Latin America.

Don't make the uneducated mistake of thinking that Latinos are "basically Mexicans". Even Mexicans come from a wide variety of education, job skills, cuisine, ethnicity, skin color, language and religion.

The common thread

While Latinos in the U.S. are too diverse to form a conveniently defined group, most Latino immigrants do have enough in common to form a fairly specific group. This does not mean they all want to live near each other, date each other, marry each other, work with each other, or even know each other.

Law enforcement and public safety officials eventually discover that the local Latino community is actually a loosely affiliated (or unaffiliated) cluster of cultures that don't mix well. The Dominicans may stay at arm's length from the Hondurans. The Cubans may despise the Mexicans *and* the Mexican radio station. And for sure, the Cubans have an enviable advantage in that they usually are not subject to deportation if they succeed in making the journey across the ocean from Cuba to Florida. Puerto Ricans are free to move between their island and the mainland as members of a U.S. commonwealth.

Still, Cubans, Puerto Ricans and other Spanish-speaking Latino immigrants share many things in common. Because of this, millions of them form the group I call "Latino immigrants", those who have entered the country during the past 25 years or so as teenagers or older.

Life as an Immigrant

The "Latino immigrant market" is a much more definite target. That doesn't mean all Latino immigrants will fit into it, but most will. In fact, we have an unbelievably large number who still fit this category and have been here for 30, 40 or 50 years. They still haven't merged into mainstream society. It's almost as if they recently arrived. A lot of Americans would be surprised and disturbed to find that these immigrants get along quite well without English by sticking close to their communities.

The following issues and characteristics help define the "Latino immigrant market".

What to call home?

This can be a heart-breaking subject of identity. Everyone needs an unmistakable place to call home. What do you do if your parents brought you here in your childhood and you hear citizens complaining every day about immigrants? This is a really, really painful pinch. It leaves you feeling unwanted, with a frightening future, feeling inadequate and outclassed, feeling confused, angry and sad. One spunky Latino song writer sang (in Spanish), "I'm not from here, I'm not from there. Like it or not, I'm going to succeed."

What do you do if you are the parents of such children? A lot of Latino parents cross their fingers and hope for the best. They have their hands full with carving out a new life in a new land against all kinds of resistance.

Rules can change fast, too. I was interpreting in court when a judge gave me instructions for two defendants. I told the judge that the governor had just handed down a rule that was contrary to the judge's instructions.

She was grateful to know, and immediately gave me new instructions. The new state rule was that undocumented immigrants—and anyone else without a valid social security or approved identification number—would be denied driving privileges.

That change triggered sudden chaos in family and work life. To get a taste of the severity of it, imagine living without your car for a week. You call a friend to take you to work in the morning. You stand at your door the next day, waiting and hoping your ride shows up. You know you're disrupting your friend's schedule. You wonder if you're straining the relationship after asking for the same favor several days in a row. Fellow workers wonder why you're not driving yourself. Maybe your boss hears about it and wonders what's going on. You get a call from home saying that you need to leave work early, if possible and if you can somehow find a ride, because your daughter has a high fever with vomiting and the school wants her taken home right away. On and on the problems go. Transportation affects your employment, your social life, your family responsibilities.

Letting undocumented immigrants establish themselves and their families and then suddenly pulling the rug out from under them is not practical or just. The very first principle in reaching the immigrants is understanding that *they are your fellow human beings*. That principle is a stumbling block for millions of our citizens.

Of course, not all Latino immigrants are here illegally. But the immigrants grow tired of hearing non-Latinos bash Latinos. They know that many non-Latinos suspect any Latino of being here illegally. Most Latino immigrants have friends and family that have not yet obtained legal status. They hate listening to the constant complaints against immigrants, legal or illegal. They're trying to put down roots and establish themselves in the face of an already complicated set of challenges. They're looking for a home.

Caring for family in the old country

What happens when a loved one back in the old country dies or is very sick? Sometimes life gets so daunting it boggles the mind. Somebody has to take care of your kids if you can't afford to take them with you to your home of origin. Or maybe you can't even afford the plane ticket for yourself. Maybe your father dies before you can say a final goodbye. Maybe your mother falls every day because you can't be there to help. Maybe you are plagued with guilty feelings, even though your parents gave their blessing for you to move to the new country. And maybe your grandpa comes from Bolivia to visit you and has a heart attack and dies and your family doesn't have the money to pay the astonishing costs of preparing him for burial and flying him back home.

These are a few of the problems that can arise when you are far from your native home. Yes, it's "part of the territory," but it's tragic when it touches you.

Problems with neighbors

How do you handle a serious problem with neighbors if you're the immigrant in their land? What would happen if you called the police? Would you be taken seriously? If you are undocumented and have been treated unlawfully (illegally) by the neighbors, will the police provide protection and assistance, or will they turn you over to Immigration? If you find yourself face to face with unjust or unkind neighbors, will you have the vocabulary and skills to speak on equal footing?

These are some of the concerns that arise in neighborhoods. The hostility can overflow into the children's lives as they walk around the neighborhood, try to socialize with other children, or try to survive in school. The stress can be unbelievable and even life-changing. It can be pointless and unending. Just think of the confidence you win with a family of immigrants (and all their family and friends, such as I) by supporting them when they go through times like these.

Who can you fall in love with?

If you are legal but the other person isn't, what pitfalls are there? Is there a future in the relationship? What do you do if you yourself aren't legal? A person's place in life can change in an instant if certain things go awry. You might find yourself in the middle of a deportation transaction for a rather minor incident, or this might happen to the one you love. Or immigration policy might be lifted or revised for a while and there may be no danger of deportation at all.

But other surprises can arise. Your sweetheart might receive a notification from her employer that says the company has been bought out and from now on everyone must present a valid social security number or tax identification, or be fired.

Maybe you get injured on your construction job and there's no insurance to pay for part of your hand surgery. Now what? You were planning on being so careful that you'd never need health insurance for that job. You were dreaming of getting married, supporting your wife while you raised a family, and now you're wondering when you're going to get married and whether you'll be able to find a job without having a valid I.D., after your hand heals.

In my book, *Dating Latino Immigrants*, I detail some of the hurdles and pitfalls that must be anticipated, addressed and overcome when immigrants are trying to find a life partner or trying to navigate life with the one they marry. Many immigrants and their spouses or sweethearts are blindsided by realities that come with starting life over in a new land.

Regardless of politics, if you want to deal with the Latinos on a humane level, you have to imagine the frequent hardship so many of them face. I know a Latino U.S. citizen who has spent his entire life in this country, except for the years he served overseas in the United States Army. He has experienced unkind treatment from our citizens who considered him a despicable foreigner. He quit speaking Spanish years ago, hoping he would be less recognized as a Latino. His Spanish is so rusty now, he can speak it only with effort. His story is one of thousands just like it.

Immigrants share many other concerns, but I hope you get the general idea that restarting life in a new land comes with challenges that most of us don't have to think about. Education is another big issue. I'll address it in the next chapter as an example of how inhumane we can become when we confuse decency with political positions. We need to know when to filter politics out of our relationships.

SEPARATING POLITICS FROM RELATIONSHIPS

Some advocates think you need to change your politics in order to relate to the Latino community. This is naïve. As I interview and converse with Latinos around the country, I find that

- They are personally opposed to the notion that people should be allowed to enter another country without permission.
- They believe immigrants are illegal if they enter illegally.
- They would like a chance to get ahead and to escape poverty, dangers, and a desperate future. They have been taught that a person should work for a living and not mooch off society.
- They believe God should be honored, even if they don't honor him.
- They believe in having fun.
- They have a wide range of political positions.

Activists often pretend to speak for the Latino community, saying the direct opposite of what individuals tell me in confidence.

Are "alien" and "illegal" offensive words? Contrary to what some advocates say, an undocumented immigrant is rarely offended by the English terms *alien* or *illegal* when they appear as general reporting in the news. In Spanish, *alien* is rarely used and *illegal* is by far the most common term for undocumented status. *Illegal* is used in songs, movies, poems, and public conversations—all of these in Spanish.

However, the words ARE offensive when used in name-calling. *Illegal* is the word of choice for referring to undocumented status, but not to the character of a person.

Many citizens have taken to branding illegals as "criminals", so as to demand an emphasis on the fact that the immigrants broke the law by entering without permission. This is a wild position to take, because most people who cross the border illegally are not dangerous, whereas we have plenty of citizens engaged in illegal and harmful, dangerous activity every day. I know citizens who have committed murder and haven't spent a day in jail for it. I've known many, many other citizens who are a constant danger to society. Most people who enter the U.S. illegally will never harm a flea. Don't call them criminals if you want to win their confidence. Don't think of them as dangerous people if you want them to take you seriously.

Understanding the children of immigrants

Americans often say, "We're all immigrants." This is to show an awareness that most of us have descended from newcomers. That is a healthy attitude. And yet, the saying makes almost everyone on the globe an immigrant, and as a result the word loses meaning. We need to understand that many children of Latinos and other groups find themselves in a particularly uncomfortable and unworkable immigrant experience that the rest of us don't pass through.

I'm talking about the children of illegal immigrants or of immigrants who brought children of a certain age into the country without proper authorization. Don't call or think of these children as illegal aliens. They eventually become painfully aware of their status. They are here by someone else's choice. You have an opportunity to help them survive, if you want to. The circumstances are too complex to spell out here, but these children are—at the present time—subject to different restrictions according to their age at the time of entry.

The Democrat Party took a divisive approach with the proposed Dream Act during the past several years. We need something less divisive to solve certain problems for the children of illegal immigrants. If you think about how children are always being told to do well in school so that they will be prepared for the future, you can see that children who cannot easily get access to college will eventually lose motivation for trying hard in middle or high school. They hear their peers talking about which college they plan to attend, usually with financial aid of some sort, and what their majors and minors will be, but they themselves don't have the same access under current law.

This isn't about everybody "deserving" to be able to go to college. The word "deserve" has its problems. But we're going to have major problems with kids who have no hope, kids who continuously see their peers moving ahead in life without them.

While Democrat politicians were adding unnecessary extras to the proposed Dream Act, making it all the more controversial and harder to pass, most Republican politicians spent their time resisting the opportunity to show they at least understood the kids' predicament. They apparently thought more immigrants would go back to where they came from if their children could be made as miserable or benefit-free as possible.

The kids are eventually going to become voting adults, because there WILL be an amnesty of some kind and there WILL be a path to legal status. Amnesty is inevitable, call it what you want. We cannot afford a perpetual subclass of undocumented immigrants, and they are not going "home". Subclasses cost society in too many ways when they are suppressed. The younger immigrants must be accepted into the mainstream as soon as possible. Kids have to be taken care of so that they can become valuable citizens.

People cannot continue coming into the country at will. Immigrants admit that we can't even let everyone stay who has already crossed. But we also cannot let people cross the border illegally by land and air for years and years, let them establish themselves and their families, and then expect them to go back to where they came from.

Restricting border crossings is not as hard as politicians have said. I have known for years who's coming across the border illegally, how many others arrive with them, how much they pay the smugglers, what happens along the way, and how and where they enter. The government knows the same thing about many others and could easily reduce the flow of immigration substantially, if officials decided to.

It should be easy to see that many children of immigrants are put in a bad position. Their lives are senseless puzzles created by unsystematic border policies. But you don't need to change your politics to relate to the Latino community. Democrat and Republican voters alike are angry about our government's way of handling immigration. Voters would like to see order, but a disorganized border policy will always be with us. It has always been part of America. It's part of the way the country deals with the demand for foreign labor and with the sticky issues that come with getting along with foreign governments and restless populations. And, of course, it's about getting the immigrant vote, even while infuriating citizens.

This chapter is an exercise in common sense for the businessperson who wants to have a relationship with Latino immigrants. Instead of taking angry political positions, you can insist on orderly immigration policies as a voter, if you wish, while you put yourself in the immigrants' shoes and and try to understand the world they live in, the challenges and concerns they regularly face. They are not going home. Get over it. They don't believe in disorderly immigration policies any more than you do. Most of them don't expect something for nothing. They have responsibilities to tend to, dreams to fulfill, sorrows to carry, life to enjoy!

Don't be distracted by the couch potatoes who come here to leach off our social services and don't want to work or buy anything with their own income or make positive contributions to society. We have an oversupply of citizens just like them, and we don't need more of the same. But they manage to slip through.

A word about who owned this land

Latinos have been in what is now the United States since before the country was formed. Some Mexicans and activists say that, when Mexicans sneak into the U.S., they're just returning to the land that was once theirs. Most Mexicans will admit that this claim ignores a few important details.

First of all, at one time or another the land was claimed in part by Spain, France and England. So you never know—maybe they'll come back and say it's theirs too. When Mexico declared its freedom from Spain, it claimed for itself the lands beyond Mexico that Spain had claimed in what would become the USA.

Secondly, the Mexican government did not ask the indigenous nations in those many regions (approximately one third of present-day United States) if they would like to belong to Mexico. Some people will say, "You cannot be illegal when you're only returning to the land that was yours. You cannot be illegal if you're entering land that was stolen from you." Yet I have not met one member of an Indian nation who thinks the tribe or its land ever belonged to Mexico. Never ever.

In summary, many nations have claimed the land. Even tribes (indigenous nations) had a long history of taking over another tribe's homeland. To this day, many American Indian nations hate each other. One Mexican immigrant told me, "The indigenous people lived in peace with each other." That is amazing ignorance. That man should at least know the violent history of the Toltecs, Aztecs and others from his native country.

Nevertheless, the people of Mexico are without a doubt some of the most wonderful people in the world. They are spectacular in many ways, and I am in my heart 50% Mexican.

ZORRO'S FAMILY SPEAKS ENGLISH NOW

Sarah de la Cruz isn't fluent in Spanish and doesn't look very Hispanic, but her grandmother's great uncle was the Robin Hood of El Dorado, whose real name was Joaquín Murrieta, who lived during the California Gold Rush.

Zorro!

Many – and maybe most – of Zorro's relatives on this side of the U.S.-Mexico border speak very little Spanish nowadays, but Sarah insists this hardly means their family identity is lost.

"I don't consider it a loss at all," says the great-great-great niece. "The change in language is more of a transition. Instead of living in Mexico, my family's lineage moved to the United States. I wouldn't move to France without learning French. Speaking less Spanish than my ancestors doesn't make my heritage any less rich or less full of stories and culture."

And stories there are. Different versions of Joaquín Murrieta sprang up over the years as his reputation after death became more and more fictionalized in folklore and media.

The real Murrieta came to the U.S. from the northern Mexican state of Sonora. Sarah's family members there and here remain in touch. This often means crossing the border and then crossing their language gap with a little help from each other.

Zorro's descendants naturally like watching Zorro movies.

Sarah said it's "quite exciting when I see connections between Zorro and my family. My mother told me that when she was younger she asked my grandmother if they were related to anyone famous. My grandmother then told her about my great grandfather's uncle being Joaquín Murrieta. When we first saw *The Mask of Zorro* in 1998 and their usage of Joaquín Murrieta as a character, it pleasantly surprised us!"

Señora de la Cruz does not glorify her Uncle Zorro's notoriety. She was raised, after all, to obey the law, and Uncle Zorro was known to break it regularly.

"What I find appalling is how people hold Pancho Villa in such high regard," Sarah said. "He killed my great grandmother's brother because he would not cooperate and allow Villa to rob the bank where my grandmother's brother worked. Yes, Pancho Villa was a revolutionary for the Mexican people, but he was a murderer and criminal who felt entitled to his spoils from pillaging."

Another Joaquín

I asked Sarah if people believe her when she tells them she's Zorro's niece.

She doesn't think so, but she says her family history is more than Zorro. "I haven't told as many people the story about being related to Joaquín Murrieta as I have of my great grandfather, Joaquín Tena Murrieta, who I believe has an equally exciting past."

That Joaquín was a politician in Sonora, Mexico, held in high esteem. Sarah said her great grandfather "was closely connected, even friends, with General Álvaro Obregón during the time of the revolution. I've heard stories that he was even asked to run for President of Mexico, but I'm sure the fact his friends were assassinated left and right if they dared run against Obregón for the presidency was one of the main reasons he didn't."

Joaquín Tena was eventually "sent to the United States because he refused to comply with an unethical request from the governor of Sonora." He was appointed to the Mexican Consulate in San Diego to administrate the Mexican department concerned with fish, game, and produce.

He later settled in Nogales, Arizona. There he met two famous actors, Robert Taylor and Gary Cooper, who were on a hunting trip to the sister city – Nogales, Sonora, México. They may have sought extra clearance from Tena, as such help can go a long way when crossing an international line.

According to Sarah, anyone who knew Tena's name "was able to cross the border without issue." Her mother still has pictures of the encounter. One shows Taylor and Cooper with their guide outside Tena's house. The guide turned out to be a Nazi spy who was keeping track of who entered or left the United States. Sarah says, "My great grandfather's story really is my favorite so far!

Don't Judge a Book by Its Cover

Sarah says heritage is more than a person's face: "You should never judge a book by its cover, because you don't know the family history and stories behind that person. I'm an American with a melting pot of cultures behind my heritage. Mexico and Spanish just happen to be the largest portion. Even my English roots are exciting, dating all the way back to coming to America on the Mayflower."

The children of Zorro's niece will have more Mexican blood than she does: "My husband is half Mexican, a quarter German, and a quarter Irish. I am a quarter Mexican, mixed in with German and many other origins. Yet one of our sons looks just as German or Irish as a native to those countries (blue eyes, strawberry blond hair), and is named Luis after my husband and his family."

Señora de la Cruz doesn't want people to underestimate her son's identity on the basis of his appearance or name. "He is an American with a rich heritage behind him," she said.

Sarah's and Her Mother's Spanish

The Spanish language came down on the maternal side. Sarah's grandmother did not pass the language on to her children, but that hasn't kept Sarah's mother from connecting the genealogical dots and maintaining family connections.

Sarah said, "My grandmother wasn't enrolled in any special programs to learn English. She was immersed in the language and had to learn it herself. She completely embraced the American culture and never taught her kids Spanish. Again, that doesn't make our heritage any less exciting. We have routine visits from cousins in Hermosillo, México and would never have reconnected with them without my mother's passion in our genealogy."

Sarah's mother lovingly threatened "my grandmother once or twice that she would never be allowed to see her grandchildren if she didn't speak to us in Spanish. But that was the extent of it. My mom laughs that my Nana would speak to us for about five minutes in Spanish and then switch back to English."

Elementary and junior high school in the Rio Grande Valley of Texas brought Sarah the option to study Spanish. She loved it, and her mother, who wishes her parents had raised her to be bilingual, supported Sarah's interest. Sarah continued learning Spanish in high school and college.

"But," she said, "because I've never been immersed in the language, my abilities are still limited. Nevertheless, when family from Hermosillo comes to visit, I can speak with them and we help with each other's difficulties in English or Spanish. We all have a lot of fun practicing!

"I find myself to be my only obstacle, for not practicing more. If I were a professional athlete and stopped practicing and working out on my sport, I couldn't expect to play at a competitive level."

Heritage Intact – with or without Spanish

Sarah emphasized that she has not lost her heritage by losing touch with Spanish.

"My heritage has always been what it is and that's not going to change," she said. "My mother and I make tamales at Christmas as a tradition along with cookies, and I plan to pass that on to my children. I've been trying to teach my older son Spanish. My children will know where their family comes from. They will have connections to that family through visits and the gift of technology like social media. So their heritage is still very rich and alive."

To Zorro's niece, the shift from Spanish to English in the family on this side of the border was a practical matter. It was simply "a characteristic of transition." If the language slips farther away from Sarah through disuse, she says it's her own fault. But, as far as she's concerned, her heritage remains intact.

What You Must Remember

People like Sarah – and there are perhaps millions of them – have (1) a strong sense of Hispanic or other roots, (2) a strong conviction that immigrants should speak the main language of the new country, and (3) a favorable attitude toward the language of the old country.

As Spanish and other languages continue dying household by household in the United States, more children of immigrants are intensifying their claim on their heritage. They proudly combine family history with their citizenship, and they see no conflict in doing so.

By contrast, people who lose touch with their roots, or who choose to do so, often think that U.S. citizenship requires a loyalty that throws out language and identity of the old country. This position is disadvantageous for businesses, organizations, and politicians who want to reach immigrants and the children of immigrants represented by proud Americans like Sarah and her family.

REACHING THE LATINOS

I've told business owners in all kinds of niches how to reach the Latino immigrants without speaking Spanish. After I explain how it works for their particular niche, these business owners are usually excited to start—but hesitant to take the first step. Therefore, if you're willing to take that step, you'll be ahead of them.

What you need to do is (1) focus on immigrants as fellow human beings, (2) communicate welcome messages, and (3) automatically distinguish yourself as one of the few in your market who care about immigrants (without needing to say so).

Roll out THE WELCOME MAT. That is, do everything you can to make sure that immigrants know they are safe with you, valued by you, that you will treat them honestly and will personally attend to them.

Here are examples of statements that "roll out the welcome mat."

- My mother's father came here from Greece. I know how hard it was for him to make a home in a new land. Here are some great coupons to use at our store to make life a little easier for you. Bring your kids in and we'll give them a nice welcome package. I promise they'll like it.
- Tell me about growing up in the old country. I love to hear those stories.
- Would you bring me a recipe for one of your soups? I'll give you one of mine.

- I know you've been in the U.S. for a while. I want you to know that I'm glad to meet you and I'm glad you're here.
- I'm going to a ballgame and I have tickets for your family and five of their friends. Please accept my invitation and be my guests!
- Tell me how to pronounce these words right.
- Tell me how to pronounce your name right.
- You know so much more English than I know Spanish. I admire you.
- I want to dress like an Argentine tomorrow. Tell me what I need.
- What are you doing on Thanksgiving Day?

You can say hundreds of specific things for your particular niche in your ad, newsletter, phone recording, signs or personal conversation. You can put them in Spanish or English or both. It depends on your particular location.

To help you stay focused, I will wave five red flags that call attention to mistaken advice that ad departments and marketing firms give about Latinos, and what you should be thinking instead.

(I'll use the terms *Hispanic* and *Latino* interchangeably.)

The 1st Red Flag Is:
"Hispanics are the fastest growing market in the United States."

This is bad and worthless advice because it gives the illusion that a Latino market exists. You can, of course, get millions of Latinos to unite on survival issues like work visas, driving privileges, and access to college. An understanding of their concerns and survival needs is what allows you to reach any sector of these Latinos.

Good advice: Carefully define the group you target. *A "Latino market" doesn't exist.* If you want to miss it, just aim at it. If I were to tell you that English-speaking Caucasians are the most populous group in the U.S., that wouldn't be terribly useful marketing information. Break it down, break it down.

The 2nd Red Flag Is:
"Knowing Spanish is critical to winning the Hispanic customer."

This is bad and worthless advice because, even though there are obvious advantages to knowing Spanish, smart businesses and organizations can work around most of them.

Good advice: If you aren't fluent in Spanish by now, it is almost CERTAIN that you never will be. Learn how to make use of the abundance of bilingual Hispanics who can fill the language gap for you. It's an insult to millions of Hispanics living in the U.S. that anyone would think they can't speak good English, when they often speak two or three languages fluently.

The 3rd Red Flag Is:
"Hispanics feel that they are treated better by Hispanic providers of goods and services."

This is bad and worthless advice first of all because it implies that Hispanics prefer Hispanic providers. Some people will interpret it to mean that a Hispanic business has an advantage. Others will say it means that you need Hispanic employees. It's also bad and worthless advice because the term "Hispanic" is too general a term to make sense of the statement in the first place.

Good advice: While many Hispanics are acutely aware of widespread bad feelings toward them, they are ready to give nonHispanics a chance. *They respond intelligently to good, honest marketing.* They are willing to compare the value and reliability of people and goods and services. Hispanics have been ripped off time and again by Hispanics. If you know how to roll out a smart welcome mat at the door of your business or organization, you can attract ANY Hispanic group that is appropriate for you.

The 4th Red Flag Is:
"Family is the cornerstone of Latino society."

This is bad and worthless advice because it can cause you to waste resources on ads that have nothing to do with the way many Latinos actually live.

Good advice: All kinds of population groups in the United States have loyal, strong family identities. What makes Hispanics superior in this way? Nothing. And they don't claim to be superior. If you have them in your family and among your friends, as I do, you already know that some Latinos have a strong family heritage and others don't. Latino families have as many problems as any other population group. They are always talking about it in Spanish.

The 5th Red Flag Is:
"Hispanics prefer doing business with bilingual staffs."

<u>This is bad and worthless advice</u> because it's a lot like saying Spanish is necessary to communicate effectively with Hispanics.

<u>Good advice</u>: The main thing is to notice the word *prefer*. The truth is that almost all Latinos prefer to do business where business is conducted well and where understanding is on both sides of the table. Keep in mind that, especially if we're talking about Hispanic immigrants, what they prefer is doing business with people who will help them navigate their new world. In addition, remember that a large number of Spanish-speakers strongly prefer that you *not* speak to them in Spanish if their English is better than your Spanish. Many value the opportunity to be involved with non-Hispanic citizens who will help them adjust to society, whether you are a fellow employee or a vendor.

Distinguish yourself as one of the few
(without ever having to say it)

Take intelligent steps toward the Latino community and you will automatically set yourself apart from the citizens who rant and rave against the immigrants. Don't eliminate yourself by believing that a "true American" takes a tough stand against immigrants. Stay focused and be sincere.

Don't eliminate yourself by thinking you have to become fluent in Spanish. The Spanish language will continue to die in this country. The Spanish-speaking population will decrease as children of immigrants go through their school years. Spanish will die as the families of immigrants age. Time will see to it. Simultaneously, the number of English-speakers will go on increasing.

Millions of Latinos already speak perfect English. Millions more are learning it fast.

"That's what I tell people!" José Gonzalez-Parodí told me. He's vice president of La Voz de Indiana, the state's only bilingual newspaper.

"And you know, the funny thing is that, if you go to the car dealerships, you'll see Latino parents there and their kids are interpreting for them."

The secret to really connecting with the immigrants lies in communicating heart to heart with concepts of critical importance to them. The children may be reluctant to recognize their roots or to discuss them with you. They may simply prefer to be recognized as full-fledged fellow Americans. But most will take notice of the respect you pay to their heritage.

Don't underestimate the Latino community. They are smart, resourceful, and inventive. They have weathered many storms, and they are cautious. They like buying things. They adore technology. They are social. They like to have fun. Offer them something of real value, with the right message, and many will give you a chance and even supply interpreters, as needed, if you handle the situation correctly.

And after you fall in love with these immigrants, you'll probably have the motivation to start learning or using Spanish words and phrases with the ones who haven't learned much English yet. They'll help you work on your pronunciation, and you can help them with theirs. Everything will be more beautiful as you cheer each other on.

They will believe in you more, because you showed the interest and courtesy to meet them partway by learning some of their language. Every time you toss in a little bit of their lingo with at least halfway decent pronunciation, they and I will know you aren't worried about Spanish taking over the country.

ABOUT THE AUTHOR

Max T. Russell has been collecting information on Latinos for more than 30 years, working with them, being related to them, and interviewing them in and outside the United States. He is the owner of Max and Max Communications.

www.ingramcontent.com/pod-product-compliance
Lightning Source LLC
Chambersburg PA
CBHW051226170526

45166CB00005B/2060